FOUND FATHERS

Growing and celebrating faith in fatherhood

NATHAN BLACKABY

With contributions from:
Carl Beech, Mark Chester, Dave Hearn,
Krish Kandiah, Steve Legg, Ian Manifold,
Jason Royce & Doug McWilliam

SECOND EDITION

CHRISTIAN VISION FOR MEN

British Library Cataloguing in Publication Data
A catalogue record for this book is available from the British Library
ISBN 978-1-912863-31-0

Cover Design by CVM

Printed in Great Britain by Bell and Bain Ltd, Glasgow

Contents

A Bit About Nathan...

Nathan knew about Jesus growing up in a Christian family but decided to follow Jesus Christ during a trip to Brazil on a church short mission trip in 2000.

In 2001 Nathan married Jennie and they both returned to Brazil, this time working in an orphanage and as missionaries with Latin Link. He also worked as a chaplain for Teen Challenge, a Christian drug rehabilitation centre in Recife, North East Brazil.

In 2011 Nathan and Jennie moved to Colchester, Essex, where Nathan pastored a church with Rural Ministries and worked as CVM's East Anglia coordinator.

In April 2014 they moved with their three young children to Derbyshire so Nathan could take up a full-time post with CVM. They have since moved back to Colchester to be near family, with Nathan taking on the role of CEO for CVM and working across the UK and beyond.

Nathan loves skipping (for exercise purposes!), motorbikes, fast cars, music and writing.

Introduction

I remember the moment my wife woke me as she moved from the sofa to the bathroom in the early hours, nudging my airbed as she passed. I woke immediately. This is it . . . this is it!

'Call the midwife!' was the order, so I did! Just hours later my life was opened to a brand-new reality of wonder, frustration, joy and love as our first baby daughter entered our lives.

Over the last few years, watching our three children grow, I have been asking myself some important questions about the sort of father I am and want to be:

- How does a father teach and train his children?
- How do I model life and my values to my children?
- How can I invest into their lives and form something that reaches beyond leaving a few quid in the bank on the day I leave this earth?

As a dad who deeply loves his biological children and also the children of others that cross over at times into our family zone, what does it mean to be this father in the light of my Christian faith in Jesus?

In my life I am trying to follow Jesus Christ, to trust what the Bible is and what it says about Jesus and to let this relationship guide me. In doing that I am tracking the journey and discovering more about my life as Nathan: husband and, importantly for this book, as a father.

To achieve this, I live my life to a CODE that helps me practically develop my relationship and trust in God. I am not talking about a dead and dry religion here that simply requires my attendance on a Sunday or my donation into the collection box as it comes around. This is something else, something that reaches deep into my heart and life and calibrates my passion, my time, my energy, my focus and my dedication. This is the CODE, known also as XII written by a great mate of mine, Carl Beech.

I:	Jesus is my Captain, Brother, Rescuer and Friend.
II:	I owe everything to him. I will do anything for him.
III:	I will unashamedly make him known through my actions and words.
IV:	I will not cheat in anything, personal or professional.
V:	I will look away from the gutter but be prepared to pull people out of it.
VI:	I will keep my body fit and free from any addictions.
VII:	I will put the welfare of those closest to me before my own welfare.
VIII:	I will treat all men and women as brothers and sisters.
IX:	I will lead as he would lead. I will honour my leaders provided this also honours him. I will follow him in company with my sisters and brothers.
X:	I will use my strength to protect the weak and stand against the abuse of power.
XI:	I will protect the world that God has made.
XII:	If I fail I will not give up. He never gives up on me.

This CODE helps me to journey this relationship and trust in Jesus with the company of my brothers and sisters. It helps me regulate my head and heart as dad when the going is good and life is on track and even the moments when I get hurt, chipped up, shot down or fail.

I want to be honest about my hopes for my children. I'm guessing that if you're a father of biological children or of non-biological children, you have hopes for them too, right? To be healthy, happy, meet someone they love and someone who will treasure them and journey life with them in a committed and loving relationship. I want grandchildren, too, even if I never get to see them. My dream is that my children enjoy these aspects of life if they desire them. But, my heart beats for more than all this, more than their happiness in the amazing privileges and opportunities this world can offer us. My aim is that they know personally the Good News of Jesus Christ. I long for them to follow Jesus, to trust him, love him and live for him.

Why?

Well their dear old dad has discovered and believes with complete certainty that this is why we've been fearfully and wonderfully made. Humans are not a pointless by-product of a cataclysmic collision of matter; our lives our created, sustained and so intricately woven that they bear a creator's signature. With this signature comes the 'why' we are shaped and formed, created and crafted in the first place. To be together, for us to be loved by the one who made us, and to love him back.

For my children, I unashamedly desire that relationship with God for them. This is, of course, their choice as it was mine. But I am asking the questions about how do I raise my kids to know their heavenly father? To trust him, follow him and live for him? Do I stick them in a good Sunday school and hope for the best?

The only logical answer to these questions that I have found is: *I have to model it.* I have to live my life in such a way that my children see the authenticity of my faith, trust and love in my heavenly father. I am not a perfect man, far from it, and at times I have to dig so desperately deep to keep my head and heart in tune. I fail, I have wrestled with depression and losing my way on a few occasions, but these paths can enable us, equip us with some of life's vocabulary that isn't bought and delivered next day; it is learnt, engrained and wrestled with. This is why the CODE is so essential: 'XII: If I fail I will not give up. He never gives up on me.'

This book is developed from two light-bulb moments I had. The first happened early one morning when I was praying for my son, Micah. I was praying that he would hear and know the voice of God in his life. I felt in my spirit that God asked me a question. Now that may seem strange; it wasn't an audible voice but a whole concept or statement from nowhere downloaded in an instant. A bit like 'I know kung fu' from *The Matrix*. Anyway, the question was this: 'Are you relying on Sunday school to teach your son to hear my voice and follow me?' Without thinking I whispered the words over my sleeping four-year-old, 'Yes, I am.'

Then it hit me, like the answer had been given but needed to be unwrapped. *'This is my job!'* I exhaled.

Sunday school played a huge role in my own spiritual development and to this day I thank God for Vince Reed, who so clearly modelled his relationship with Jesus Christ to me at Sunday school. But if you are a Christian man or on the journey, then I think it is essential that, as men, we grasp our role and responsibility as fathers in the spiritual development of children. We can't sit back with a mindset of 'send them to Sunday school, they are the professionals'. If they go to every Sunday school session a month then that's about two hours a month they will hear about 'God' stuff. You could double that to four hours a month by simply giving them ten minutes a day to pray, read a story, or for you to tell them a story that reveals something of God in your life.

This isn't only about time; I'm just giving you an example of where my head was. We have a short time in which we can influence our children and invest in their lives. But if we do – as my father taught me – the effects can stretch for generations.

The second light-bulb moment came when I read a news item claiming that almost 2 million families in the UK are 'fatherless families', and this number is increasing at the rate of around 20 thousand per year.

The fact that whole sections of society live their lives with no father present demands a response. My hope is that God will use the small contribution this book makes to start fires in the hearts of men all over the UK – that they would wake up to the importance of fatherhood to all the children in our lives. This book seemed like a good idea and then it was made loads better by some friends contributing their thinking too. The vision is simple: *to help us see our heavenly Father's call to us as men, and to be encouraged and supported in our own journey as fathers and father figures to all children.*

What does fatherhood look like to children who need foster care or adoption? How do we navigate the teenage years with our children? How do we approach the 'SEX' talk? How can we mark the process of manhood for sons? How can we *be* intentional, good fathers if we have limited contact with our children or we're in a blended family? Fathering toddlers and being a godly grandfather are all included here too.

I would like to say a massive thank you to all the contributors who gave of their experience and time for this little book. Thanks also to those who helped fund and produce the first edition of this book and FMI for helping us produce edition two.

1. Integrity (Noah)

This chapter, written by me, will be exploring a few characters in the Bible who help us navigate and explore certain elements of fatherhood. Some of you will be familiar with the stories, but if you aren't a Christian and these stories are new, you can find all these real-life stories in the Bible. Most of these men had a thread in common: they were normal men, like us, who through faith were able to live remarkable lives. So let's get this started with Noah.

Now let's be clear, Noah wasn't a perfect bloke. He messed up, he liked a glass of wine or five and ended up being seen by one of his sons in a drunken, naked mess, which caused much embarrassment and a few family problems.

But, we mustn't forget that Noah was a man who . . . sorry, the ONLY man who, amongst his peers and neighbours, refused to live a wicked and sinful life.

Now that's important. Integrity is vital in our pursuit to be great fathers and grandfathers to our children. Noah was a man who held firmly onto one thing when no one else around him did: his relationship with God. Noah was surrounded by the perverted practices of a nation living in darkness, but he refused to saturate his life with the wickedness of his day.

How often have we been with mates when the banter has become personal about the foreign bloke on staff? Or jokes start being told that belittle some ethnic group to the applause of the other blokes? What about the top-shelf magazines in the garage where you pause for a quick flash? Then there is that attractive receptionist who always seems to wear outfits you like – can you look away, intentionally controlling your eyes and your heart?

We may think no one notices this stuff, but guess what, our children do! They might not be present during these times, when we're at work and play, but they are influenced by who we are when we're around them – and the kind of men we are is revealed by these micro transactions during our day.

When I live a life outside of my home that has no integrity, it affects my home life and that's a fact. My kids don't get prayed with before bed. I don't pray for them privately, on my own, either. I avoid sitting to open the Bible and pray with my wife. Going to church on Sunday quickly starts to feel like just another thing to take up my precious weekend.

Why does that happen?

It's about intimacy with Jesus and obedience in following him. When we say 'yes' to dirty jokes, racist banter, the receptionist's revealing outfit or the top-shelf magazines in the garage, we start to say 'no' to Jesus and his way. Our lack of intimacy with the living God when we're not at home begins to impact our children when we are. But if we live our Christian lives with integrity and consistency – at home, at work, in all we seek to do – then our children will be impacted.

TAKE MY WORD FOR IT

In recent months I have been training my puppy. Leo is a Bouvier Des Flanders, and at just four months old he was already almost 20kg. I quickly learnt whilst training him that much of what I do with children is the same process, but thankfully not the poo bags anymore.

When raising our children we use boundaries to set in place a clear framework for expected behaviour and rewards. Clued-up parents know that the key to this strategy succeeding is consistency. Even when you're tired, fed up, need a break and just can't be bothered, consistency is king. But the same is true for us as we seek to become fathers of integrity. In order for us to model integrity to our kids, we need to live lives that are honest and consistent even when we think nobody is watching us.

While everyone around Noah was heading in a different direction and chasing the pleasures of the world, he refused to live a life that ignored God. He also took God at his word. This is something our children need to see us do. Noah had an intimate relationship with God in which he could hear and understand the still, small voice of God in his life. As a result, he set about building a huge boat in the middle of the desert, then waited for it to rain. No one had ever seen anything like it. From the moment Dad set about his 'building project', not just Noah but his whole family would have been subject to daily ridicule. Yet, nothing stopped Noah from doing what God had instructed him.

Not only did Noah demonstrate integrity, he modelled a profound trust in God to his family. 'Kids, I believe Almighty God has told me to build this boat and I am taking him at his word!'

I don't know about you, but I want my children to know that when Dad or Granddad thinks God is speaking and guiding him, he obeys. You can't teach this unless you're living it out. I don't think we can ask or expect our children to take God at his word if we don't.

EXPLORE . . .

The idea of shaping our integrity with God, praying and asking him to help us when the pressure is on and no one is looking, may be a new thing. Or maybe you are there but need to keep on the narrow path and holding the line.

Spend some time now in stillness and reflection before God as you read Psalm 139.

If you can, still your head from the noise and business of the day and slowly read the Psalm over. You might find it helpful to honestly express some of the frustrations you may have with particular areas of your life in which you have lost integrity.

In the space below you can write, or reflect if that helps too, if perhaps something stands out from the Bible verse.

_____

_____

_____

_____

_____

_____

_____

_____

_____

PRAYER

Jesus, I want to be honest before you. Help me to journey with you to be a man of integrity. Create opportunities for me to speak, to live and to trust you with an honest and sincere heart. Amen.

2. When Am I A Man, Dad?

By Dave Hearn

The Ojibwe, or Chippewa, were a Native American Indian tribe that lived on the shores of Lake Gichi-gami, now called Lake Superior, on the present-day border of Canada and the United States.

Their lives were simple and for the men mainly consisted of hunting and fishing (sounds good to me!) while the women looked after the children and cultivated maize and squash.

Their spiritual lives were very important to them, marked throughout their lives with ceremonies and rituals honouring the Creator. There were ceremonies for marriages, births, and the coming of age of both girls and boys.

In the Ojibwe, a father and grandfather would lead each boy through a rite of manhood. During the first part of the ritual, the father gave his son a small doll that had been created by the tribe during the boy's birth ceremony. This Native American version of Action Man symbolised the boy's childhood – his life up until then having been spent mostly inside the wigwam, playing games and taking orders from Mum. Now the boy was instructed to break the doll in half, signifying dramatically the break from his former, childish ways and his decision to follow the ways of a man. Once this was accomplished, the other men of the tribe surrounded the boy, encouraging and assuring him that he would be taught the ways of the tribe and thereafter treated as a man.

Following this emotional process, the father presented his son with a brand-new hunting knife. This knife would be used by the boy for the rest of his life, so he was commanded to treasure it, care for it and protect it with his life. The knife had a deadly edge and clearly was not a toy to be trifled with. Depending on the particular part of the tribe, the initiation might continue with tracking and hunting a buffalo or caribou.

At the culmination of the ceremony, the boy was given new clothes and told to stand in the middle of the tribal meeting ground. His grandfather or another tribal elder would give the boy a new name, announcing it loudly to the entire tribe.

He now had a new identity and was a full member of the tribe. The boy was gone – the new man had come!

The power of these symbolic acts is unmistakable:

- The breaking of childish ways
- The acceptance of responsibility, danger, maturity
- The introduction of the new man

Today, our sons struggle through adolescence, trying to come to grips with their burgeoning strength, sexuality and intelligence, while being enticed by the seemingly safe highs of sex, the escapism of video games and other destructive habits. They are often fearful of the responsibility and self-discipline that comes with adulthood. As fathers, we must help our sons through this period with strength, love and firm counsel.

But we ourselves can easily be intimidated: 'I don't know how to raise a teenage boy!' We may have struggled, or still struggle, with those temptations ourselves. So how can we guide our sons into manhood?

CREATE A BREAK FROM THE PAST

Like the young Ojibwe boy breaking his doll in half, your son needs to make a clean break from his childhood. Take him on a special birthday adventure. Make a big deal of a special gift or heirloom. Encourage him to go on a solo backpacking trek. It's exactly this break that needs to happen – from perhaps playing it safe at home to joining the ranks of the men who defend the community – that's what initiation into manhood is all about.

TRUST YOUR SON WITH RESPONSIBILITY, RISK AND DANGER

That hunting knife was no joke. Imagine giving your thirteen-year-old a knife that he could shave with, and bestowing it with such reverence and instruction that he absolutely understood the power he was being trusted with.

That type of gift might not be your cup of tea, which is understandable, but we've got to trust our sons to act with independence, to make some risky calls and to do some dangerous things. Boys must face pain and learn how to deal with it. They must go through physical and mental hardship, and experience what it's like to come out the other side. They need to know that pain exists; that they will not be able to avoid it; that their parents can't get them out of it. They need to be able to process the pain and know that there are other men who have gone through it and survived.

Here's also where we teach our sons about responsibility: household chores are a start, but a job is better. A piggy-bank is nice, but a bank account is what adults have. If we want them to be men, we've got to treat them like men. They might hesitate at first, but they'll soon understand and appreciate what it means to be treated with respect and held to a higher standard.

REMIND YOUR SON WHO HE IS

Your son's identity – and our identity, for that matter – starts with the One in whose image we were created: God. As sons and daughters of God, we have power and authority that transcends physical strength. Everything we do, everything we are, must flow from this confidence. After that, tell your son about his earthly lineage: tell him the stories of his grandfathers, the legends and the tall tales, the good and the bad. This is how we learn. This is how we pass on our DNA – not just through our blood, but through our storytelling. Let your son know who he is destined to be: speak over his life, bless him, don't curse him.

HAVE A BAND AROUND YOU

A boy's initiation into manhood was never meant to take place in a vacuum. Support and love from grandfathers, uncles, family and friends is critical.

Let him know that he has an entire 'tribe' to fall back on, who have stories and experiences that can help him as he learns. Take your son on guys' nights out, pub nights, and to sports matches. Talk to him. Share your difficulties, your temptations, your triumphs, and what it really means to be a man.

Our job as a parent is to teach and coach our children, to help them become independent, self-governing adults.

Remember that none of this is meant to hurt or abuse your son. As fathers, we are here to guide them through this growing-up process. It is scary, so a loving, firm hand is what boys need. An initiation ceremony doesn't need to involve wigwams, peace pipes and sweat lodges, but there needs to be something – a break from the past, a time of introspection, testing and accomplishment – then a re-entry into the family, not as a boy, but as a man.

Maybe you think that you yourself missed out on any kind of initiation, or that you are unable or ill-equipped to guide your son into manhood. I urge you to seek out a father – your biological father, a trusted mentor, or a spiritual father – who will lead you through an initiation.

The goal for you is to live a life with purpose, to break free from childish things, to bring life to others, and to stop living a self-centred life. If you need someone to lead you through that process, find a band of brothers that you trust in your church or community.

Here's a final challenge to fathers, no matter what the age of their sons or daughters:

Give your children everything they need. Do not give your children everything they want. Take your son into the wilderness. Teach him how to make a fire. Teach him how to change a tyre. Teach him how to treat a woman and how to respect adults. Teach him to listen more than he speaks. Teach him that he is not the centre of the universe. Teach him to fight for something that is worth fighting for.

Dave Hearn
Founder, Global Adventure
www.global-adventure.org

Global Adventure was created to provide safe and fun 'initiation' experiences for fathers and sons, and to challenge men to live as brothers. Father and Son Training events combine camping, hiking, climbing and caving experiences with teachings on developing physical, mental, emotional and spiritual maturity. Men's Adventure Discipleship events are bespoke adventure weekends for men's ministries or men's groups.

3. Commitment (Jacob)

If we are looking for advice for fathers and potential fathers, then perhaps Jacob, whose twelve sons went on to be the twelve tribes of Israel, can help. (The people of Israel, their life and historical journey is captured largely in the Old Testament of the Bible.) However, what makes Jacob so interesting is that he had a change of identity that shaped his future.

When Rebekah gave birth to Jacob and Esau, Jacob came into the world hanging onto his older brother's heel. Jacob's name means 'schemer' and 'manipulator', and he lived that out when he tricked his ageing, sightless father into giving him Esau's firstborn blessing. (You can read this story in Genesis chapter 27.)

Now let's fast forward a little and pick up the story with Jacob and Esau having gone their separate ways. Jacob heard news that his brother was coming back to see him and this sent fear and panic into his mind. By now Jacob had a few families, children, land and cattle living together. In Jacob's master plan he started to think that Esau, the brother he robbed, was coming back with a mob of fighting fellas to carry out revenge.

So Jacob split his family, sending his loved ones in different directions, hoping to spare them death at his vengeful brother's hand, and braced himself for the storm.

Then something happened. The Bible tells us that Jacob wrestled with the Lord.

Now, I don't know about you, but I am a careful driver. I make effective use of the rear-view mirror, like a radar continually scanning for danger. But I would be making a terrible mistake if I only looked in the rear-view mirror and never ahead at what was in front of me. The trouble we often have is that the events of the past have shaped us, sadly scarred us, and they loom like a huge rear-view mirror in our lives. When we try to look ahead, all we see is the past. It has a huge impact on our life going forward.

Jacob was known to his mates, his employees, his family and the guys at the local well as the cheater, the schemer. It was, after all, his name! So when Jacob heard that his brother was coming to see him, he looked into his personal rear-view mirror and saw his chequered past catching up with him again.

But Jacob met God that day and this encounter dramatically changed things. The Bible tells us that, one night, Jacob wrestled with a 'man of God' – probably an angel of the Lord – and he fought until he was told to let go! Jacob replied, 'I will not let you go unless you bless me' (Genesis 32:26).

Jacob had drawn a line in the sand. He wasn't prepared to carry on with 'business as usual' in his life until God did a transforming work in him. How do we know that God transformed Jacob? Well, let's look at what happened: Jacob is renamed 'Israel' by God. Renamed! He'd had a name which had labelled his life and coloured his future, now all of that was rewritten! In due course, as his brother approached, the two men embraced and, with many tears and much emotion, the two were reconciled. It is an amazing moment in the Bible and a great account of restoration and transformation between two brothers.

As a father I have been really encouraged by reading this account of Jacob in the Bible. In our lives we can be committed to so many different things: sport, hobbies, classic cars, the list goes on. These are not bad things. Jacob showed a deep commitment in holding onto God with all he had. That's commitment. It's like he just refused to let go of God until his life was changed.

I would love to have met Jacob. In Hebrews 11 in the New Testament of the Bible we read that whilst leaning on his staff, still limping from his wrestling encounter with the living God, Jacob prayed a blessing over his grandsons. Here we see the generations who are being influenced by a father's commitment to the trusting and holding on to God; Jacob showing his children what real faith and commitment is all about!

EXPLORE . . .

A friend of mine once told me that if we want to inspire our children to trust God and seek him, let them see you pray. Perhaps take some time to read Hebrews 11. Don't rush it; find a version you like and take your time. It might also help to listen to this chapter being read with some headphones on.

If you want to pray and think about your own life and if you have a past that feels like it's stuck in your future, use this space to write some of it in the space provided below, or how it feels.

_____

_____

_____

_____

_____

_____

_____

_____

_____

_____

PRAYER

Lord, I will trust in you. Help me to journey beyond the familiar and into the unknown. Give me the faith to leave old ways behind and break fresh ground with you. Christ of the mysteries, can I trust you to be stronger than each storm in me? I will believe you for my future, chapter by chapter, until all the story is written. Amen.

(*Prayer of St Brendan*)

4. Grandfathers

By Ian Manifold

As his line manager said to Werner von Braun when he asked for a pay rise, 'C'mon mate, it's not as though it's rocket science!' Not true, but this chapter really isn't rocket science.

Knowing what to do is easy. Really doing it is the hard bit, but it's the only bit that matters.

What does the Bible say about me being a grandfather as God would want me to be?

First, there's the general principle which should power everything I do: God gave the life of his Son, Jesus, to pay for my rescue from destruction. Jesus is my example and my 'on-board power pack' for life. How can I not live in gratitude for that? How can I not live in the strength of that, with Jesus as my role model? The more this truth sinks in, the more I am drawn to sacrificially love my children and grandchildren. My job is to be to them a visual aid for Jesus – for them to see him in me. My hope is that they grow up to serve him for the rest of their lives, whatever that costs me or them.

But the Bible also says some special things about grandparents and grandkids. Look these verses up:

- Grandkids are meant to be a blessing, an enjoyment, something to be proud of in the right way (Proverbs 17:6; Psalm 128:6; Job 42:12,16).

- Grandparents are meant to be a witness and a powerful spiritual influence down the generations (Deuteronomy 4:9; 2 Timothy 1:5).
- God gives the thumbs up to the right sort of granddad (2 Chronicles 21:12)
  (Asa was Jehoram's granddad, but I'm sure you already knew that!).
- Your life may be used by your grandkids to explain about God.
  Q: What God? Whose God?
  A: The one my dad and my granddad follow (Genesis 31:53). This was before God had made himself known through stuff like rescuing the Israelites from Egypt or coming to us as Jesus.

What a privilege and what a responsibility!

How should this work out in practice? First, I have to say that my wife Gillian and I have been undeservedly blessed with six grandchildren, aged six months to eight years. We are even more undeservedly blessed that they belong to two sets of Christian parents.

Why are my daughters believers? Because of God's kindness and, I suspect in large part, the lifelong prayers in the past of our own parents and their grandparents. I'm writing from my own experience here, but I've also spoken to a number of other Christian grandfathers. Here are some bits of heartfelt and, I hope, wise advice.

• **Be honest**

Really look into your heart and life. Decide what makes you tick and what part Jesus plays in your life. If there are big question marks, if you are play-acting, your kids and grandkids will see through you more than most.

• **Be different**

When compared to non-Christian grandparents, we need to be 'the same, only different'. Several granddads made a similar point. We just need to be great granddads from the kids' point of view: enjoying wholesome fun with them, celebrating the good things in life; sacrificially spending time with them as we are able; being interested in their interests. For one granddad, for instance, it was especially about attending his grandson's football matches.

At the same time, though, these fun, champion-at-being-normal granddads need to show their grandkids that they're not privately or publicly ashamed of Jesus and their faith in him. For example, they should answer their grandkids questions, go to church with them, say grace before meals, pray with them and read the Bible, or Bible stories, to them when they stay overnight.

We need to lay down lasting markers of faith. One granddad I know, as part of his grandkids' presents every Christmas, gives donations of animals and equipment on their behalf to families in developing nations, to teach his grandkids something of the true meaning of Christmas.

We shouldn't whinge about our church or our leaders in front of our grandkids (we shouldn't be doing it anyway). They will soak up our cynicism and gossip as much as our enthusiasm, and these mixed messages will confuse them more than they do an adult. All of this equally applies to being a Christian dad.

• **Be as present as you can be**

Being one step removed in your relationship with your grandkids, compared to your kids, can make things more difficult and complicated, especially in these days of fractured families. It may mean we feel more anxious and helpless in times of crisis. Physical distance for families who are spread across the country or the world makes this worse. But it does force us to rely more on prayer. This is good, because prayer should underpin everything in our lives. Often we treat it as a last resort because of our stubborn 'I can cope' attitude.

One friend told me that all he could do was pray for his grandkids, whom he'd never met because they live abroad, born to a prodigal son who lives a chaotic life. He's not in touch with his son who was born out of a relationship my friend had before he became a Christian. A difficult situation, but he prays on regardless.

Another friend who is involved in prison ministry said that a survey asking prisoners 'Who was the most influential person in your life?' revealed that for many it was a grandparent (especially a grandmother).

This wasn't particularly about Christians, but it shows how many grandparents are holding together fractured, troubled families over two or three generations.

• Be a standard bearer for godly values
It's great to want our grandkids to 'be happy, live long and prosper' but our primary aim is for them to know and serve the Lord for the rest of their lives. These two aims may not always coincide. We need to realise and accept that the world's mantra – 'Well, as long as they're happy' – is not our mantra.

Suppose, for example, that you have granddaughters who hold onto and practise their faith into adult life. If the church in the West carries on its trend, the chances are they may have to remain single for the whole of their lives because there will be even fewer Christian men than the minority which exists now. That's one of those taboo 'let's not preach about it' facts, but it's still a fact. Do we secretly compromise our hopes and aims for our grandchildren, or do we (and our sons) wake up and get stuck into CVM's aim of reaching a million men for Jesus?

• Be consistent and supportive
We need to exercise self-control, self-discipline and wisdom. The quality of our relationships with our children and our help and support to them as parents is crucial to our effect on our grandkids – perhaps even more so with non-Christian parents. This can boil down to simple stuff like willingly giving up our own arrangements to babysit the grandkids. We have to respect

parents' views and accept their boundaries when we are tempted (because it gives us pleasure) to spoil our grandkids too much.

We need to keep our mouths shut when we don't quite agree with the way our kids discipline their kids and we shouldn't undermine them. If we have really serious worries over this we should prayerfully and sensitively address it, one-on-one, directly with our kids, not behind their backs.

We have to be especially sensitive when parents are non-believers. Then, we have to carefully take opportunities to witness wherever we can to our grandkids; the rule is to be as open as possible with their parents and respect their wishes. Here we have to rely even more on prayer and being a good example. One friend told me about how his prayers were answered when his grandkids with non-Christian parents were witnessed to by people entirely outside the family. This issue of non-believing parents obviously matters less when the grandkids have come of age.

We need to show the same degree of love to our grandkids whether they are Christians or non-Christians, have parents who are Christians or non-Christians, and whether they are grandkids or step-grandkids, adopted or biological children.

• Be amazing!
I asked the grown-up Christian grandchildren of a Christian friend what they thought of him as a granddad. They said 'amazing' and it wasn't just a figure of speech. The reason was

his self-sacrificial, helpful, godly character (they used their own words for this). I thought to myself, 'Yes, that's just what I think about him too' – and I see it coupled with a willingness to open his mouth about Jesus.

We've talked about how grandkids are influenced by us but, as we get older, we move more and more towards being on the receiving end of help from others, rather than the giving end. This is difficult for our pride and independence, but it's all as God intended.

A Christian friend told me how his grandkids were the first to arrive to support him when their aunt, his childless daughter, suddenly and tragically died young. What goes around, comes around.

Ian Manifold
CVM Chairman

5. Love (Isaac)

One of the things you will often see if you are connected to social media is the prolific use of 'life mottos'. You know, the type of thing that makes you cringe and 'un-follow' whoever it was that posted it! Well, despite all my criticism, I stumbled across one that I liked. A young son is asking his father how he will ever find the right woman to be his companion in life. His father replies, 'Son, don't look for the right woman, just focus on being the right man!'

I liked that. No, I mean I actually 'liked it' with the thumb. (It's a Facebook joke.) Okay, moving on . . .

My son Micah is continually watching me. In his early years almost every moment you could see him filtering his life through mine. He copied the words I used, the things I wore and the way I relaxed. He was right there with me. (It's changed a bit now he has discovered online gaming!) But if I grabbed a stick on a walk he immediately got one too, and I loved watching him discover his world through his dad. If I hit a tree, so did he, and on we go.

A few years back, I was outside the house adjusting the chain slack on my motorbike. I'd got my tools set up, the bike on the axle stand, and had started working. I looked around and there was my son and one of my daughters with their toy bikes. They had their wheels in the air and had both helped themselves to my tools. In their world, they were doing an F1 pit stop, like dad.

Silently, I just watched them and almost took a deep breath. Our children are watching us in micro detail, what do they see us do, how do they see us react, what do they hear us say or watch?

I found this a sobering, humbling moment. My son and my daughters are watching my wife and I and asking themselves the question: 'Who am I and how should I be?'

There is a story in the Bible of a family who started to journey with God a long time ago. Isaac was Abraham's son, and was under massive pressure to live up to the family name and be like his dad. (Abraham was a man who walked with God in a close relationship and became a father to many nations.) Abraham must have seen that in Isaac, a young boy growing up, watching his father's every move. We read in the Bible that Isaac even copied his dad's moves when he was worried about his wife Rebekah's safety. He lied to the Philistines about her, a play his dad had made twice! But as Isaac grew, the Bible tells us about a moment in his life when he was out walking alone through a field, meditating. It was here that he met Rebekah, looking up to see her approaching with some camels and from then Isaac loved her deeply and she was a comfort to him (Genesis 24:63–67).

I think that Isaac's meditation is significant to us as dads, grandfathers and fathers of the future. I tend to either be out at work or living in the business of a hectic home with my wife and three children. I rarely get to be home alone on my own, with no noise or demands on my time. So I often grab half an hour to just walk, often with the dog. Whilst walking alone through fields, the land still wet with dew and the sun just starting to come up, I have found moments of stillness, full of awe at the amazing scenery around me, and have been able to meditate on the Bible in surroundings that inspire a profound sense of God's presence.

I cannot prove to you that this was also the case for Isaac, but I know that God uses experiences like these, when there are no distractions, to get our attention. The Bible tells us that in that moment of meditation and stillness, Isaac looked up and saw Rebekah approaching. It had all been arranged by God's sovereign hand.

Isaac lived at a time when human society accepted the fact of polygamy and yet we read that he devoted himself to Rebekah in every way and loved her deeply. As fathers who have an audience continually reading us like page-less books, we must be aware of how we treat the women in our lives and, in particular, our wives or partners (singular!)

Our daughters are asking questions about how men should treat them; about the qualities they should look for in their future partner. Our sons are asking questions about the type of man they will be; how they will treat women; how they should go about investing themselves deeply into these relationships.

When and where are they asking these questions? All the time they are watching us!

How we behave is providing them with answers. Of course, we are not the only input into our children's lives, but we are and should be the most significant.

My hope is that my daughters will see the deep and sacrificial love I show my wife; that they will see the time spent to understand and value her, to encourage and strengthen her life and faith. This commitment to my wife demonstrates to my daughters the kind of loving, caring relationship they should aspire to and the expectation they can have of a man who follows Jesus. For my son my hope is for him to learn how and why he should love in this way, which has its unbreakable root in my relationship with the living God.

Isaac deeply loved only Rebekah in a time when he didn't really have to. He chose to take her into his heart and by doing so modelled to his children a fantastic lesson in love.

EXPLORE . . .

Spend some time now in stillness reflecting on 1 John 3:11–24.

Take time reading this section of the Bible, maybe find somewhere outside where you can reflect on it. Read it a few times and invite God to help you process it in response to this chapter.

You may want to use this section of the book to write a few thoughts and notes to these questions:

In what ways have you been shown and understand love?

What has been the most loving thing that has impacted your life?

_____

_____

_____

_____

_____

What practical steps can you take to clearly demonstrate the love you have for your family? Spend some time praying for your family.

_____

_____

_____

_____

_____

PRAYER

Jesus, please give me wisdom to know how to lead my family along the right path with love. Help me to show my child/ children how to love, even when it hurts. Thank you, Jesus, that you love me, even when I fail to realise you are there. Thank you. Amen.

6. Men Fall In Love

By Doug McWilliam

Whatever the reason, being separated from your children is tough. When a marriage or partnership has ended and the kids are somewhere in the middle, caught between you and mum or even a third party, they are going to be confused and hurt by the separation. This will also be true for you.

If your relationship ended because it didn't work out and you find yourself divorced and single, this will be painful, but it does not mean that you have divorced your children. You love your children and you are going to have to work out a new type of relationship – one which includes how best to have access to them. It may be possible to accomplish this amicably, or you may face some hostility, but however the arrangement works out there is one thing you can be certain of: you are your kids' father; they are your flesh and blood. You fell in love with your kids once and forever the first time you set eyes on them and you want the best for them.

We all make mistakes in life. We all get things wrong and have to bear the consequences of our actions. Some men, through guilt or shame, treat this as an unhappy life sentence, while others positively rationalise their circumstances and find constructive outcomes. This latter group don't beat themselves up every day. Partly, this has to do with how we understand forgiveness and know how to deal with guilt. We need to learn how to forgive ourselves. The Bible teaches us in Psalm 32:5

that if we confess to God what we have done, he will forgive the guilt of our sin.

Our feelings will be put to the test, but there is something very positive about discovering that set against all the emotional, spiritual and physical upheaval of a break up, we are not really a 'bad guy'. Sure, there are times when we are stretched to breaking point and we don't deal with it well. Then we feel like we're the bad guy. We may have even been told that we're a bad guy because of the break up or divorce. Yet, there is still an inner voice that says we're not really a bad guy. What does a 'good guy' look like? What makes him tick? It's important to understanding one thing and hang onto it if nothing else works: *you have to love your kids with no strings attached.* Being in love with his kids is one of the best experiences a man has in life, so focus on that. Concentrate on loving your kids to the best of your ability, with God's help. This is a good start on the road to feeling positive about yourself. It will help you focus as you rebuild your life.

BEING CONSISTENT

Your kids will build their own understanding of what happened to their parents' relationship as they try to make sense of the world around them. In this regard, your role is no different than it was when you were together/married: to be a positive role model to them. You can still have a profound, positive effect on your children, despite the circumstances. You still have a key role to play in shaping their lives.

Following the break up they will be confused about their relationship with you, how to relate to you, and how you relate to them. They will be confused about the nature of love. Subtly, they will be observing how you feel about yourself and how you feel about them. Your kids read you like a book, so when the time comes for access to them, your appearance, behaviour and speech are all important. You need to be true, genuine, and express your continued love for them.

When relationships become fractured we have to re-learn how to look after ourselves. You still have a life to live, so live it in front of your children and make it good. Don't become a slob. It's easily done: you don't exercise, you drink too much and eat junk food. Keep your integrity. It won't do your kids any good to see you having a string of new, short-term relationships or, alternatively, shouting and storming because you don't have a relationship. You can tell your kids that you love them until you're blue in the face, but they won't believe you if they see that you're incapable of loving yourself. Your kids need to see that being a 'good guy' is demonstrated by loving yourself, loving them, and also remaining secure in their love for you.

Work at living a godly, disciplined life. It need not be complicated. Cook for yourself and your kids, do your washing, make and keep good friendships, keep fit, read books, pray, read your Bible.

In everything, Jesus is our role model. Sent by his Father, Jesus came into the world. He wasn't born into opulent luxury, but arrived poor in a world that was hostile and disenfranchised, suffering from deep brokenness. For all his amazing personal qualities, Jesus wasn't accepted. He was a good guy, but that didn't stop the world from trying to get rid of him. Jesus experienced the ultimate tough love. He left the place of complete love and acceptance in his Father's presence to hang on a cross, with immense pain and suffering, bearing the sin of the entire world. During that blackest moment, God his Father was not there for him. He was cut off and cried out to God only to be answered with silence.

Equally, God at that moment knew what it was like to be cut off from his Son. This is important to know for Christian men who have experienced a break up and who have limited time with their kids: God knows what it feels like to be cut off.

Jesus constantly took time out to talk to God. As he journeyed, he got together a group of men to travel with him – his buddies. These men were both fun and challenging. They were the ones he could be intimate with, sharing his feelings. He even took the brave step of telling them he loved them.

In the same way, God loves you with an unadulterated, feely given love. As you return this love to him, something amazing happens. You find a unity with God the Father and you begin to be made whole again. Jesus overcame sin and rose again to be united with his Father. He promises us unity with God and with himself. Trust yourself to trust him.

The quality of your life is central to all your relationships. To be the best for your kids demands a new focus, born out of a deepening relationship with God. Sacrificially give your time to them. When you're not with them, plan your time with them so that it's constructive and has a beginning, a middle and an end. Make that time count!

Here are some top tips for maintaining a stable relationship with your kids:

- Don't promise anything you can't deliver.
- You set the boundaries and you maintain them. If you don't, your kids will know you're cheating them and when you come to hand them back they will have learned not to trust you. So much for loving your kids!
- Be on time. Your kids don't need to be swamped by lots of gifts; what they want is to be with you – dad and kids together. Develop a range of activities that are relational. You may think sitting watching TV together is relationship building, or spending four hours in the cinema will do it. No, it just fills in time till your kids go back.
- Learn to do those things that give you eye contact, like reading together, walking or running about, playing in the woods, etc. Help them with their homework, pray and read the Bible with them, go to church. All these things demonstrate the values that you want in this relationship.
- Be in conversation. Keep in touch with your kids. Keep talking and listening.
- Remember that you are a good guy. You are building your relationship with your children and working to make sure

you have quality time together. Through this your kids will know that they are loved and you will be loved in return.

- Show yourself some tough love when you're feeling miserable, fed up, things are not going well and you're being blamed, money is short, etc. You still love your kids, so love them through all the trials. After all, it was not their choice to be caught up in your everyday life. Allow your love for them to transcend your circumstances.

- Remember that you can still demonstrate a quality of life to your kids that will feed the quality of their lives.

Above all, remember that forgiveness is God's gift to us. We all make mistakes, but with repentance comes God's forgiveness. If he can forgive a murderer, he can forgive you for a broken marriage. Don't be weighed down by guilt, but allow forgiveness to become central to your life and relationships. Jesus paid the price for your freedom. Love your kids and love yourself – because you are a good guy.

Doug McWilliam
Youth and Community Worker/Trainer

7. Honesty (Joseph)

The story of Joseph in the Bible makes for some fantastic reading and study. We might know of Joseph because of his famous coat of many colours, given to him by his dad, Jacob. It was a lovely coat that turned heads, but unfortunately for Joseph, it was the last straw for his brothers, who could no longer take Jacob's devotion to his favourite son. Of course, Joseph himself made the problem worse by sharing a few dreams he'd had with his bros. Again, it didn't go well.

An astonishing truth about Joseph is that, by living a life of honesty, he found himself in some really bad situations. But, we don't see Joseph giving up and wishing he had never spoken or lived out the truth. Instead, we see him trusting in God even through the storms.

Honesty can be a difficult thing to use wisely and helpfully. Joseph 'honestly' shared his dreams with his brothers. They turned out to be authentic, prophetic dreams foretelling events to come, but that wasn't the point. These pictures of his family bowing to him were like salt to an open wound. They stung!

Joseph, on the back of these revelations, soon found himself at the bottom of a dry well, stripped of his posh coat and abandoned by his brothers. They lied to his father about him, saying that his son was dead, sold him to some travelling merchants and moved on with their lives.

Joseph ended up in Egypt, working for one of Pharaoh's officials, a man named Potiphar. The Bible tells us that the Lord was with Joseph so that he prospered. This is interesting. The Lord not only blessed Joseph, but everything around him. His master Potiphar, the workers and animals, all flourished because of Joseph's relationship with the living God.

My wife, on occasion, eats sardines in the home. I have tried to protest about this and stage uprisings against the consumption of sardines in our abode, but all my efforts have been cut short. What does that have to do with Joseph and honesty? It's simple. When you open a can of sardines something happens. It releases a smell that has the capacity to penetrate all rooms, clothing, hair and, well, your life! When my wife eats her sardine sandwich the house stinks. The carpets and curtains stink, my clothes and hair seem to absorb the smell. When I leave the house, it follows me!

I want to suggest that a godly father/grandfather who holds honesty in the palm of his hand, will see the influence of its 'fragrance' wherever he goes. His home, his family, his work, his relationships, his passions, his public and private life, will carry the fragrance of honesty and, I believe, God's blessing.

We read that Joseph was a well-built and handsome guy, something that did not escape the attention of Potiphar's wife, and it wasn't long before she had invited Joseph to the bedroom for sexual relations.

Now let's be clear here, Joseph was a bloke, muscular and handsome, and would not have been unaware of the pressures blokes face in relation to attraction and sex. Time and time again Potiphar's wife literally invited him to a banquet of adultery but the Bible tells us that he rebuked her every time and avoided her in every way.

If you know someone has some degree of attraction to you, you might have found that your mind creates scenarios of how this could play out. You find yourself thinking about it. Why? Well, because it makes you feel good. Someone has seen the goodies and likes what they see! You might even start to make conscious efforts to show that person how good you look in your best shirt, or to be funny or charming in order to continue the 'game'.

Joseph was having none of it. Right from the start he told her 'no'. Not because of the responsibility he had to his boss, Potiphar, but primarily because he had an intimate relationship with the living God who had called him to walk in holiness. Bam!

In the end, Potiphar's wife cornered Joseph alone and made a desperate play for him. The scuffle ended with Joseph fleeing the scene, and then her lies began. The story goes on and Joseph got banged up in prison for his honesty. For around two years he was inside and guess what? God was blessing him again, even in prison. There's no record of Joseph complaining about his mistreatment. The narrative just tells us how God used him to reveal the hidden truths in dreams.

In the end, after being sold as a slave by his family, lied about, imprisoned and forgotten, even though he'd done nothing wrong, Joseph was summoned by Pharaoh because the ruler had had a dream. Joseph interpreted the dream through divine inspiration and once more we see Joseph, the man of honesty, blessed by God and eventually reunited with his family.

The point is: God had a sovereign plan all along. Joseph can teach us a lot about honesty and how we handle it.

EXPLORE . . .

Open your Bible at Philippians 4:8–9 and spend some time in prayer before you start.

What does 'honesty' in your life look like?

_____

_____

_____

_____

_____

Reflect quietly on the following areas of your life and the honesty that you are living . . .

- at work
- at home
- in your social life
- in your private life

Have you felt that even though you have lived honestly, God has been quiet in your life? Write something about that here.

_____

_____

_____

_____

_____

Spend some time in prayer bringing your frustrations before God and, if you can, share them and pray with someone you trust.

If you have sensed that a lack of honesty has impacted your life, list any situations or moments where this has been true in the space below and bring these in prayer to God.

_____

_____

_____

_____

_____

PERSONAL REFLECTION

If you don't know the story of Joseph, then read it, but the point here is that, as godly fathers, our honesty in life is essential. As we seek to be Christlike, our honesty in our public and private lives will be a fragrance that impacts our family. How do we apply any of that? Ask yourself a few questions about honesty and how you use it. The Word of God revealed to us by the Holy Spirit is like the rule of honesty for us. As you read and pray ask the Holy Spirit to illuminate areas of your heart and life that need honesty; that need a new commitment to truth. Now start to practise it, little by little, moment by moment.

8. Steps To Father

By Krish Kandiah

Every time I speak at a church, afterwards I always seem to have a queue of women waiting to chat to me. They are not drawn by the seductive fragrance of my anti-perspirant or my stylish, slim-fit shirts, or even my magnetic personality. No. These women are queuing to tell me that they feel a call on their lives to offer love and care to vulnerable children through fostering or adoption. Invariably, however, the first obstacle they meet is their husbands. What should they do?

I have to admit that it was my wife who first felt passionate about fostering and adoption in our family. We'd had three children in three years, were still in our thirties, and by my calculations our child-bearing efficiency meant that my wife and I would maximise our time together before we got too old to enjoy active life together. Don't get me wrong, I absolutely adore my children, but I was consoling myself that when we became empty-nesters our home could be a love nest again. We could do all those romantic things like taking city breaks, having long lie-ins and watching sunsets together – like we should have done before we had children, but never did!

So when my wife, Miriam, said that she felt God was asking us to open our home to lost and broken children who'd had the worst possible start in life, I thought it was good theology but a bad idea. I thought it was a worthy calling for other people, just not for us. Looking back, not for the first time in our marriage, my wife was completely right and I was completely wrong. Every objection I put up was basically driven by my selfishness.

Six months down the track it was my turn to be right. It was a difficult and emotional process applying to become foster parents and there were many times when Miriam may have pulled out, but I was able to inject some perseverance and determination to help get us to the point where we were finally approved.

Fostering and adopting children is one of the most difficult things our family has ever done, but undoubtedly one of the best. As soon as God opened my heart to the needs of these children, his Word came alive to me in a different way. I realised there were whole chunks of the Bible that I had ignored and I came to appreciate God as a Father to the fatherless and protector of widows and orphans. As I learned to love and help and advocate for vulnerable children, I connected to God in a whole new way.

So much so that I want to share the privilege with other men. Let me give you three reasons why you should at least consider becoming a foster or adoptive dad.

GOD DEMANDS WORSHIP THAT IS MORE THAN SINGING AND READING THE BIBLE

I must admit, I get bored quickly singing worship songs and even sometimes listening to preaching (especially when it is me doing the preaching). Somehow we have turned worship into something we do for an hour or two each Sunday in a church building or a school hall. That was never God's intention. The Bible clearly states, 'Religion that God our Father accepts as pure and faultless is this: to look after orphans and widows in their distress' (James 1:27). There is not a lot about singing or preaching in that definition of true worship, is there? But that is just one verse and, theologically speaking, proof texts are not a great way of reading the Bible. There is not enough space for me to quote the whole of Isaiah 1:1–17, but if you look it up you will see that the James verse is not a one off. In fact, now I've pointed it out you will notice every time you read your Bible, God keeps reiterating that worship that doesn't lead to care for the vulnerable isn't worth anything.

Take a quick moment to MOT your worship of God. If it doesn't have some component of care for the vulnerable, it is probably defective.

Unfortunately, a monthly donation to a worthy cause probably doesn't cut it. Chances are, the priest and the Levite who walked past the man who had been attacked by robbers on the Jericho road were probably doing a better job than you and I on tithing their income and they still were criticised by Jesus for not showing the kind of love that the good Samaritan demonstrated. Fortunately, the answer is not singing more sincerely or going on a pilgrimage to the other side of the world – it is simply and actively sharing our lives with the vulnerable on our own doorstep.

KIDS IN CARE END UP IN SOME DARK PLACES WITHOUT US

I love the fact that the UK church is involved in helping people through wonderful things like prison ministry, supporting people caught in the sex industry, offering debt advice, giving hungry people bags of groceries and helping the homeless.

But the truth is, many of these same people the church is helping could have had very different lives if only someone had fought for them and protected them when they were young children in the care system. Children who come out of care are overly represented in the sex trade, in prison, rehab centres and in our homeless populations. Why don't we get involved in their lives when they are three years old and in need of a loving home, instead of waiting until they get in trouble in their twenties and thirties? Ask any one of them about the father figure in their lives and I have no doubt that what you hear will make you cross or bring you to tears, or both.

So I am not asking you to consider whether or not you want children or extra children in your life, I am asking you to consider whether you could be a father to a child who needs one. Adoption is not supposed to be a last-ditch option for couples who can't have children naturally; it is a last chance for children whose lives will be permanently scarred and skewed without someone who will give them a home where they can be loved and encouraged.

YOU WERE BORN TO MAKE A DIFFERENCE, NOT JUST TO MAKE MONEY

I know there is a certain amount of satisfaction to be gained from bringing home a pay cheque at the end of the week or month. But what truly satisfies is when you are doing what

God created you to do: loving him and loving your neighbour, showing the world the character of your heavenly Father – a Father who fights for his children, who loves them, who teaches them, who rescues them, who forgives them and who blesses them.

With 6,000 children waiting in care for an adoptive family and another 9,000 foster families needed across the UK, there is a pressing need for Christian men to step up and play their part.

It isn't all giggles, eating KFC and watching footie together (although I have some great memories of a seven-year old foster son who was the only person in my family who loved Liverpool FC more than I did and correctly predicted that we would stuff Arsenal 5-1 before we sat down to watch the game with my Arsenal-supporting oldest son!). It isn't all kite-flying and bike-riding, although I have precious memories burned into my mind of faces properly lit up after giving a couple of boys those amazing first experiences. It cost me nothing but half an hour of my time in the park across the road, yet it meant everything to those boys at that time, and the pleasure and satisfaction it brought me was priceless.

Those smiles become even more precious when you know what terrible backgrounds the children have had. They carry heart-breaking stories, physical scars and emotional wounds that may never go away.

This is not a calling for the faint of heart or faint of faith. Fostering and adoption is extreme parenting and is not for everyone.

Perhaps, after considering it, you will decide you need to support somebody else to do it, because you can't. But humbly present your home to God as a potential refuge and ask him if this is what he wants you to do – ideally before one of the women in your life starts challenging you to do it.

If you are up for finding out more, 'Home for Good' is a little charity a friend of mine and I started, quitting our secure jobs at the Evangelical Alliance to get it off the ground. We are recruiting foster carers across the UK to act on the frontline of supporting children coming into the care system.

We are also pioneering a new route to adoption for Christians that promises to value your faith and to give you the best support adoptive carers can get in the country. Drop me a line at krish@homeforgood.org.uk or phone our helpline: 0300 001 0995.

Krish Kandiah

Dr Krish Kandiah is founder of Home for Good and the President of the London School of Theology. He is married to Miriam and they have three birth children, an adopted daughter and anywhere between one and five foster children living with them. He may occasionally 'over share' on twitter @krishk
www.homeforgood.org.uk
www.lst.ac.uk

9. Strength (David)

David is perhaps one of the most well known of the Bible men, but how can he inspire us in exploring fatherhood?

David was a man who knew the bitter disappointment of personal sin and failure. At one point in his life he allowed the roots of lust to entangle his life and deceive his heart into following his own desires and plan. He soon found himself covering up an adulterous relationship that had resulted in pregnancy by orchestrating the death of an innocent man. What a disaster!

Taken in that context, David would not be a good role model to serve up to our children. In fact, if this episode from his life was reimagined as a TV soap, it would swiftly be turned off. But despite his failings, David discovered strength in God and this is something of great importance to us today as fathers.

We don't need to read much of David's life to know that he had the heart of a warrior. David knew the taste of battle. His hands were skilled in battle and his courage and fearlessness were unmatched. In today's society we have people writing books about how to rediscover a heart of masculinity; about the wildness of the male heart. Without serving up a hot potato here, let's simply conclude that if these books are out there it's because they need to be – and millions of men are reading them!

Now, I'm not calling us men to forge a makeshift sword in the gas fireplace at home and show real courage in the battle for masculinity. What I am suggesting is on a different path altogether. David discovered that real kingdom strength is never found in our physical or mental accomplishments.

Look at the story that unfolds in 1 Samuel 24, where David is being chased by Saul and no less than three thousand men. It's a long story, go and read it.

At one point, David and his men are taking refuge deep in a cave. As it turns out, Saul pops into the very same cave looking for somewhere quiet to go to the toilet, and is unaware of David's presence. David creeps up on Saul, sword drawn, and cuts part of his robe. He could easily have killed Saul, but David feels a heavy conviction over cutting the robe of God's appointed leader. After Saul finishes his business and leaves, David emerges from the cave and calls after him. David runs to Saul and lies face down in the dirt at his feet, unwilling to lay a hand on him.

So David had the chance to take Saul out – the man who was trying to kill him – but he wouldn't do it. He refused to rely on his own strength to resolve the situation. This is because the real strength in the life of David was his relationship with the living God.

In Psalm 51 David confesses his failings to God and gives some incredible glimpses of this strength that we can learn from.

'You do not delight in sacrifice, or I would bring it; you do not take pleasure in burnt offerings. My sacrifice, O God, is a broken spirit; a broken and contrite heart you, God, will not despise.' (Psalm 51:16–17)

God confirms his heart on this issue in Psalm 50:9–13.

> 'I have no need of a bull from your stall or of goats from your pens, for every animal of the forest is mine, and the cattle on a thousand hills. I know every bird in the mountains, and the insects in the fields are mine. If I were hungry I would not tell you, for the world is mine, and all that is in it. Do I eat the flesh of bulls or drink the blood of goats?'

This is not about how animals were sacrificed, God didn't really need them anyway. What he really wants is us! David nails it when he says that what God is looking for is a broken and contrite heart.

This flies in the face of men battling out their masculinity by forging a path with muscle and brute force. Godly men are men who know that without God they are in spiritual bankruptcy! Nothing in the bank, no hope, no plan, no future, no nothing!

Just verses before David calls out to his Lord: 'Create in me a pure heart, O God, and renew a steadfast spirit within me. Do not cast me from your presence or take your Holy Spirit from me. Restore to me the joy of your salvation and grant me a willing spirit, to sustain me' (Psalm 51:10–12).

We are called into battle; we are to rise up and be men of this generation. But at the core of this army is a contrite and broken heart that is daily restored by the grace and strength of Jesus Christ.

If we are to show our children strength, let it be his strength shown in our weakness!

EXPLORE . . .

Spend some time in prayer and invite the Holy Spirit to speak to you as you explore this study. Read Psalm 28.

What do you think your strengths are?

_____

_____

_____

_____

_____

Honestly summarise your commitment to personal times of prayer and study of the Bible.

_____

_____

_____

_____

_____

If your family described you to a stranger, what would you want them to say about your faith?

_____

_____

_____

_____

_____

Spend some time in prayer to refocus your mind on the source of your strength and ask the Lord to bring a greater intimacy to your faith in him.

PRAYER . . .

'Create in me a pure heart, O God, and renew a steadfast spirit within me. Do not cast me from your presence or take your Holy Spirit from me. Restore to me the joy of your salvation and grant me a willing spirit, to sustain me. Then I will teach transgressors your ways, so that sinners will turn back to you.' (Psalm 51:10–13)

10. An Awesome Kind of Dad

By Mark Chester

I am in awe of Joseph, the father of Jesus. Put yourself in his position for a minute.

He is a young man in love with a beautiful woman, whom he will soon marry. He's excited, optimistic, looking forward to sharing himself, mind, body and soul with this pretty girl called Mary. He's an honourable guy, so he's saving himself for the marriage bed, but he can't stop thinking about the time when his patience and restraint will be rewarded and he will, at last, be able to make love to Mary.

Joseph is filled with hope and electrified with anticipation but then Mary delivers some crushing news: she's pregnant! How does he react? What does he feel? Anger . . . hurt . . . resentment . . . bitterness . . . sadness? I suspect he feels broken and wounded – the pain of intense betrayal. But Joseph has a quiet integrity, so he plans to do the right thing, avoid any unnecessary drama and break off the engagement in the most low-key way possible.

It's a tough time for Joseph and sleeping isn't easy. His constantly churning thoughts are keeping him awake. Even when his body manages to sleep, his mind doesn't. One fitful night he dreams about an angel. It's a vivid dream and the angel's words are clear: the baby was conceived by God and Joseph must still wed Mary. When the baby is born, Joseph must name the boy Jesus and become his father.

Here's what I'm thinking: if this is God speaking, and Joseph must have had his doubts, he's expecting a lot. He's asking Joseph to risk his status, reputation and happiness on the basis of a dreamt notion that this is what God wants him to do! How does Joseph respond?

He does exactly what God's angel has told him to do and becomes the earthly father of the greatest man in the history of the world.

Joseph's example teaches me a lot about being a father and emphasises the importance of being involved in our children's lives straight from the off. Firstly, it's important to note that Joseph was not Jesus' biological father. I believe that we must apply all the principles of good fatherhood not only to our own biological children, but to all children. We must accept and respond to the truth that we are the 'fathers of many children'. If we embrace this the way Joseph did, then we will surely have the best chance of passing on our faith to the next generation.

I love the fact that Joseph treated Mary with the utmost respect, even when he must have contemplated the possibility that she had been unfaithful to him. I'm sure there were some tricky conversations between them but, still, Joseph 'did not want to expose her to public disgrace', and he planned to call off the wedding quietly.

It reminds me that a good place to begin being a good father is to love and honour the mother of my child. I know that this is a huge challenge when a relationship has broken down, particularly when there is disagreement and wrangling about practical arrangements, but if we can maintain civility and respect, we begin to teach our children how to relate to others in a way which brings a greater sense of inner peace.

The fact that Joseph had his doubts about the future of his relationship with Mary shows that he was as human as you and me. But this guy believed in God. I mean, *really* believed in God. When he dreams that God's angel tells him not to be afraid of marrying Mary because the baby is from the Holy Spirit, Joseph believes it to be true. That must have required a whole lot of determination. Like Joseph, we have to be determined to believe. When we are wracked with fear or doubt or desperation, when all else fails and we hit rock bottom, we have to fall back on a determination to believe that God is there.

The starting point for our children's faith is a belief in God and they will only believe in God if they know someone else who does. If we want our children to believe in God and walk with him throughout their lives, we have to show them our faith from their first days onwards. As their fathers we need to demonstrate that we will not abandon our journey with God for any price.

Joseph risked his status, reputation and happiness, but he wasn't playing fast and loose. He did it based on what he thought God was telling him to do. Nevertheless, his safer option would have been to break things off with Mary and find another girl to marry. No one would have blamed him.

People must have been whispering and it would have been a way for him to alleviate the personal sting of the rumours. But Joseph chose to ignore the gossip and take a risk. What a great example to set for his son, an example that said, 'Don't always play it safe, son. Don't conform. Be resolute in what you believe and take a risk on the basis of it.' Joseph's belief resulted in action and he swam against the tide of popular opinion. His son grew up to do the same thing.

Joseph certainly got involved in family decisions. He twice moved his wife and son – once to Egypt and then from Egypt to Israel and Nazareth – in response to more angelic appearances in his dreams. He was a man taking responsibility for the spiritual direction of his family, and doing all he could to guard the safety of his loved ones. Joseph was a protector, but he didn't feel it necessary to exercise physical prowess to protect his young family. Instead, he flexed his spiritual muscles. He listened to God and he obeyed.

It encourages me that we fathers can all play the role of protector for our families, regardless of our height, shape or the size of our brawn. We can do it by seeking the will of God and finding the courage to follow it.

Joseph was concerned for his son. When Jesus was twelve years old, Joseph and Mary discovered that he was not with them as they journeyed back home from Jerusalem, so they began to search for him, retracing their steps. When they found him in the temple courts, Mary scolded him: 'Son, why have you treated us like this? Your father and I have been anxiously searching for you.' Clearly, Joseph thought about his precious child and inevitably those thoughts sometimes grew into worry, just as you and I worry about our children. We can't afford to be passive when it comes to our children's lives. Their early years will pass before we know it and showing our interest in them will become more difficult as they get older and choose to spend their time with others. So we must think about our children, consider their characters, speak to God about them, ask ourselves what's best for them and make sure they know that they are on our minds and in our prayers.

I've saved the best until last because I love the part where Joseph and Mary take the baby Jesus into the temple courts and the righteous and devout man, Simeon, takes Jesus in his arms and praises God for him. The Bible tells us that Jesus' parents 'marvelled at what was said about him'. Joseph was pleased with his son. Being a father brought him joy and delight. We, too, should delight in our children and show them that we do. They are a gift from God and deserve to be appreciated and cherished. Like Joseph, we must allow ourselves to marvel at what we see and hear. Each time our children feel that we, their fathers, are pleased with them, it is like giving them a jab of emotional adrenaline. Our children need our approval. It's clear to me that Joseph's heart was turned towards his son and when a father's heart is turned to a child, I believe there is spiritual power at work.

At my church, Hoole Baptist Church, Chester, in March 2003 we began to specifically reach out to the fathers and children of our community in the hope that we would help turn the hearts of the fathers to their children and the hearts of the children to their fathers (Malachi 4:6). We set up a Saturday morning parent-and-toddler group called *Who Let The Dads Out?* Other churches replicated what we did and came up with ideas of their own. The *Who Let The Dads Out?* movement began to grow. In 2012, the Bible Reading Fellowship (BRF) became the custodians of the movement and we continue to work to inspire and support its growth and development.

Throughout the UK and beyond, churches are welcoming dads and children across their thresholds and giving them the opportunity to have fun together, share some food and create happy memories. We cannot introduce people to the goodness of their heavenly Father unless we first know them, and *Who Let The Dads Out?* is an opportunity for churches to do just that – to get to know the fathers of their communities, turn the hearts of those fathers and their children to one another and open the way for God's power to begin working in their lives.

Joseph is the kind of father we hope *Who Let The Dads Out?* will encourage a father who believes in God, is courageous, a risk-taker, a survivor, a protector and a father who marvels at the gift of his children. A father after God's own heart.

Mark Chester
Founder, Who Let The Dads Out?
www.wholetthedadsout.org.uk

Who Let The Dads Out?, *a core ministry of BRF, began in 2003 at Hoole Baptist Church, Chester, and has grown into a national movement of churches which are reaching out to fathers, father figures and their children.* Who Let The Dads Out? *groups are catalysts for developing friendships and sharing faith.*

11. Wisdom (Solomon)

The life of Solomon is a life that was, without doubt, filled with everything the world (at that time) could offer a man. If the fastest camels had been available, Solomon would have had four of them in different colours with private number plates and all the accessories.

Solomon's wisdom and wealth were no secret. His fame and reputation the cover story, the centre article and the back page, bringing glory to God (1 Kings 10). The Queen of Sheba heard about Solomon and rolled into town with her entourage. When she arrived with all her clever questions and gifts she was literally in awe and overwhelmed. As the Queen of Sheba looked at Solomon and all that God had done, she had to acknowledge the Lord of all wisdom and life who was working through his vessel, Solomon: 'He has made you king to maintain justice and righteousness' (1 Kings 10:9).

However, somewhere amidst this endless pursuit of material accomplishments was a fault line, an unseen fracture that had been covered up for years with the veneer of public success. The private victories in the life of Solomon of obedience to the Lord were, unlike his father David, coming up short.

Solomon had been instructed, along with the rest of the Israelite community, not to marry women from other nations – foreign women. The instruction from the Lord was rooted in the shaping of a people, a nation who were in a covenant with him to be his people and he their God. Marrying outside the

Israelite community would introduce false gods through these non-Israelite spouses and fracture this deep bond and the identity the Israelites had as the people of God.

But Solomon nurtured a love for foreign women, some 700 wives to be exact, plus 300 concubines (usually a female sexual partner who was unable to be taken in marriage) and this was a major problem.

The simple guideline that God had instructed Solomon to live by, for the protection of his relationship with God, was broken and the results were catastrophic. Solomon's heart was turned away from the living God by his collection of foreign wives and he established the worship of Ashtoreth – a tree trunk carved and placed into the ground.

Solomon had been used by the Lord to strengthen Israel geographically and spiritually as he built towns, whole communities, a temple of worship and a palace to live in. He built an army and a fleet of ships that returned to Solomon on one occasion with sixteen tonnes of gold. King Solomon did things big – the temple and the palace, for the time, were epic. When Solomon dedicated the temple he made a burnt offering of 22,000 cattle and 120,000 sheep and goats. Amazing stuff! But how did it all go so wrong for Solomon, a man gifted with heavenly wisdom? The Bible records a wonderful moment in the life of Solomon, because let's not forget, like many of these founding fathers, they had ups and downs in their lives. Solomon, in a heartfelt prayer to the Lord says:

'Now, LORD my God, you have made your servant king in place of my father David. But I am only a little child and do not know how to carry out my duties. Your servant is here among the people you have chosen, a great people, too numerous to count or number. So give your servant a discerning heart to govern your people and to distinguish between right and wrong. For who is able to govern this great people of yours?' (1 Kings 3:7–9)

What a fantastic prayer from Solomon. He didn't ask for wisdom in all things – i.e. how to achieve personal fame and glory – he asked for wisdom to know how to lead the people in his care.

However, even with all that wisdom Solomon was unable to see the fault line appearing and deal with it well. As Solomon began to lean into his own understanding and wisdom, the crack began to surface and divide a once intimate relationship. The wisdom which Solomon received from the Lord was never intended to be a 'one-time only' filling of wisdom.

The heart of this prayer, containing the metaphor of a little child, was lost as Solomon became independent, thinking he knew how to lead without the Lord.

Imagine how Solomon's story could have turned out differently if it had been about him continually seeking the Lord, daily falling on his face to return to the only true source of strength and wisdom.

In John 15:5 Jesus points to this truth, saying, 'I am the vine; you are the branches. If you remain in me and I in you, you will bear much fruit; apart from me you can do nothing.'

Solomon got distracted and forgot to 'remain'. He lived an incredible life, asked for wisdom and got it, but with all this wisdom failed to see that he needed the discipline of a daily, obedient life before God.

One of the things I am doing for my children is to keep a book – three books in fact, one for each of them – in which I record things for them. These aren't things that I can't tell them to their face, but things they might miss along the way. I have moved my family on many occasions, changed schools, homes, friendships, countries and so on, so the purpose of these books is to one day look back to see how their dad was trying to live a life dependent on the Lord; that all the stuff we experienced as a family wasn't about my own efforts or wisdom, but about walking through daily intimacy with Jesus in obedience to him. These books will hopefully speak, when I failed to, to show my children, like the Queen of Sheba discovered, that behind the man's wisdom is a faith, trust and hope in the living God and his glorious Son, Jesus.

EXPLORE . . .

Take some time to read Solomon's dedication prayer at the new temple (1 Kings 8:12–21). Read the two psalms written by Solomon (Psalm 72 and 127).

What areas in your life do you feel you need wisdom?

_____

_____

_____

_____

_____

What do you think wisdom from God would look like?

_____

_____

_____

_____

_____

Now read James 3:13–18. In a few words summarise godly wisdom.

_____

_____

_____

_____

_____

Spend some time asking God to lead you forward in godly wisdom.

PRAYER . . .

Lord, thank you that you are my source of life, wisdom and hope. Help me to trust you every day, to lean not on my own ideas, but to look to you. Shape me each day to move in step with your will. Be glorified in me today, Lord.

12. The Sex Talk

By Jason Royce

If you don't talk to your kids about relationships and sex, someone else will!

I recently saw an extreme example of advertising for a world-famous seller of customised subs: 'SEX! [in massive writing] Now that we have your attention, eat at Subway.'

Sex is everywhere. It's in nearly every film from Bond to *Fifty Shades of Grey*, TV programmes like *Game of Thrones* and *Boardwalk Empire*, and endless adverts, magazines and music channels.

Sex is used to sell us stuff, get our attention, and make us feel like we're missing out. It's even portrayed as a lifestyle!

I meet very few parents who need convincing that guidance about this stuff is needed. But just in case, here are three reasons why I think you need to talk to your kids about relationships and sex.

BECAUSE GREAT RELATIONSHIPS NEED A GREAT SET OF VALUES

You want your kids to have great relationships in the future, don't you? Of course you do. So you need to be in the business of communicating your values to your children, showing them the way that you act in your relationships. There are plenty of others communicating their own values – from the media to friends and family.

In fact, it would be a fascinating exercise to observe and analyse everything that is communicated to your kids about relationships in the space of a single week. Here are some that I see cropping up in the media time and again:

'If it feels good, just do it! . . . faithfulness is optional . . . if your relationship breaks, get a new one . . .'

If you want your kids to hold different values to these, then you need to pass them on in both word and deed.

BECAUSE 1 IN 3 TEN-YEAR-OLDS HAVE SEEN PORNOGRAPHY

As I visit schools across the UK I see a worrying trend: porn is educating our young people about sex. Some know this is abnormal, but others say it is normal because everyone is watching it. I saw a quote the other day from a young man who said, 'That's the idea [of porn], to take that video and do it on a bird.' You may be okay with all of that, but if, like me, you think those ideas are bad news then we need to be purveyors of a better story. How does a ten-year-old know what to make of pornography unless someone is talking to them about it?

BECAUSE SCHOOL CAN'T TAKE CARE OF EVERYTHING

As we know, kids learn about some of this in school. They will learn about reproduction and sex in science and some schools have very good relationship education too. Other than that, sex and relationship education varies from excellent to terrible to non-existent. The most recent Ofsted reports found that, overall, secondary schools weren't teaching nearly enough about healthy relationships. Even when it's done well in schools, teachers can't provide your kids with the cultural context, values and, most importantly, love that you, their parents, can.

QUESTIONS TO CONSIDER . . .

- What values, beliefs and ideas about relationships and sex do you want your kids to hold onto in the future?
- Is sex special? Why?
- What makes a good relationship?
- How can we help our kids develop the skills they need to build lasting relationships?

SOME BIG IDEAS FOR DADS

So you need to talk to your kids about this stuff, but where to start the conversation? Here are a bunch of the best tips and wisdom collected from conversations with parents like you about what works in practice.

START SMALL AND BUILD ON IT

If you've never had a conversation about this topic, don't start by addressing pornography! Start with questions like, 'What do you think makes a good friendship/relationship?' Or tell them that you want them to have great friendships and a great romantic relationship in the future and that you're there to help them learn about it. Remind them, 'If you ever see anything online or on a friend's phone/tablet that you don't understand or want to chat about, I'm here and I won't judge you.'

Remember that they already know a lot about what you believe about this topic because they've seen you act in friendships and relationships. Our example is so much more powerful than our words (but still use both example and words!). Tell them about your experiences, both good and bad. Tell them about relationships you think are good. Tell them about great women and men who you look up to.

Remind them that you've made mistakes and are still learning too.

ASK QUESTIONS

Don't fall into the temptation to deliver your best hour-long talk on relationships and saving sex until marriage. Keep it until they ask! In the meantime, commit yourself to asking the questions you think would be helpful as they interact and interpret the world around them, and listen long enough to hear the answers. For the record, 'Don't you think that listening to your parents' advice and doing as you're told is important?' is NOT a question!

Instead, try questions like, 'What have you found difficult recently?' or 'What's been your highlight of the week?' or 'What have you thought about most this week?' and keep going with the questions. Over time you'll deepen the level of communication and trust.

THE RELATIONSHIP BANK ACCOUNT

I meet a lot of dads who have had 'the talk' with their son or daughter. I know that many of them would rather have taken a bullet than had that talk, but they did it anyway. The question I have for them is: why do we build it up so much? It's like we think we only get one shot at it and we expect it to go BADLY – badly enough so that neither they nor we will ever want to repeat it.

We put too much pressure on handling this conversation flawlessly on the first occasion. From the dads I speak to each week I can tell you that it's not likely to happen, but it doesn't matter anyway.

THE PLAYLIST

A friend of mine went to his son and said, 'We both know I'm not cool. I'd love to learn about some music that is cool! Could you make me a playlist?' His son did. Whilst he didn't like all of it, he learnt about what his son was interested in.

If you take a genuine interest in what your children are watching, playing and listening to, you'll notice your relationship with them deepen and you'll have more to talk about. You'll also know what questions to ask.

DON'T COACH ON GAME DAY!

I ran a football team for eleven years. I was very passionate and would jump around with excitement and shout instructions from the side lines, such as: 'Pass the ball! Keep it simple! Have a go!'

One of the dads, watching for the first time, came up to me before a game and said, 'Well, this is it! You get to see whether your coaching has made a difference. The coach's work is done on the field of training, not the day of the game.'

Those words have stayed with me ever since.

I realised that I was still coaching on the day of the game. I needed to let them learn by playing the game. I was there to support and guide them, but they needed a bit of space to grow.

There can be the temptation to go into 'helicopter parent' mode for this child you've cared for since it was born. You rightly desire to protect them from danger and even from themselves! You want to help them with every decision and make sure that they always make the right choice. But with every passing month of their life, they're striving for autonomy – or, sadly, becoming so dependent on you that they'll struggle to do much for themselves.

Remember you are parenting for long-term results. You are doing your best to raise well-rounded humans who will experience success and have great relationships. Keep this in mind as you interact with your offspring. The results of successful parenting are lifelong – it's not all about what happens before the age of eighteen. Give them some space to grow! Not all at once, but bit by bit help them to enjoy and take responsibility for their freedom. Be there to support and guide, but increasingly let them decide when they will utilise your help.

GO AND HAVE SOME FUN!

A friend's daughter was asked by one of her peers, 'How come you have to spend so much time with your dad?'

She said, 'I don't have to, I want to!'

I hope you have a lot of fun having these conversations with your kids and that they enjoy it as much as you do. It may take time, but stick with it and you'll get there.

I'd love to hear how you get on. I can be contacted via the website below.

Jason Royce
Romance Academy Director
www.romanceacademy.org

We're a youth movement making a stand for healthy relationships and wisdom when it comes to sex. Our innovative approaches make the important conversations fun and frank, and they are always packed with practical tips. Why not book a member of our national speaking team to come and inspire your young people, congregation or group?

13. Listening (Samuel)

The Bible tells us in James 1:19 that we should be 'quick to listen, slow to speak and slow to become angry'. There is a lot of wisdom in that! So often we want to speak and share our thoughts (we are experts on everything), to push our ideas, to make sure we get our voice heard and, to be honest, that seems to be the way the world works. We are encouraged to speak up, to be heard and have a voice, and of course that's right, but listening is something intentional, something extraordinary.

I remember once being part of a training seminar where we had to sit face to face with someone and listen to them for five minutes. Just listen. We could nod and encourage the person speaking with some facial expressions that showed them we were still with them, but that was all.

This type of exercise is over the top to make a point, but the art of listening is something we fathers need to look into.

Communication with our children is so important and as my children are growing I sense the need to sharpen my listening skills all the time.

There are a ton of self-help books on how to be a better listener and how to communicate well with your children . . . I am not an expert in that, so get yourself to a library. However, there's also some good and bad news.

The good news is that God wants to talk to you and your children all the time, to develop intimacy, trust and obedience. In hearing and knowing his promises, his love and faithfulness, the wondrous work of salvation will be shown in your life, your generation and that of your children.

So what's the bad news?

Well, it's up to you to help teach your children to listen and respond to the calling of Jesus in their lives and this requires sacrifice and commitment from you. Samuel had been committed to serving at the temple after his mother, Hannah, made good on her promise to God and had dedicated him to serve the Lord under the High Priest, Eli. One night, Samuel was resting in his bed. Eli was an old man who often needed some help and Samuel, who was around thirteen, was on stand-by for the ageing man.

During the night, Samuel heard a voice calling to him, so he rushed out of his room to attend to Eli and made relevant inquires as to his need. Eli had no clue what the lad was on about and sent him back to bed again. This happened again and again. Samuel heard the voice calling him, he got up, and Eli sent him back to bed. Eventually, Eli realised it was the voice of the Lord and that he wanted to speak to the young boy Samuel. So Eli told Samuel that the next time he heard the voice speaking he was to say, 'Speak, Lord, for your servant is listening' (1 Samuel 3:9).

Samuel went back to bed and the next time he heard the voice calling to him he responded as Eli had instructed. The Lord spoke and Samuel listened.

This was great news for Samuel. He lived at a time in history between the last of the judges who guided the Israelites and the kings who reigned over them. Samuel was God's man and he knew how to listen to the Lord.

Samuel had received wise and discerning instruction from Eli during his life and it had shaped and nurtured him. This came at a cost to Eli, who was essentially training up his replacement. Eli knew his time was short and an investment had to be made into the next generation.

Also, Eli was discerning in some aspects, but drastically undisciplined in others – shaping his own sons, for instance. Eli had been warned already about his wicked son's ways and when the Lord spoke to Samuel that night, the message he delivered was that Eli's bags were packed! Go check it out for yourself!

So what can we learn here?

Recently, my eldest daughter made some big school transitions. She is going through a challenging time and this is naturally reflected in her behaviour at home.

After spending some time praying about it, I really sensed that I needed to help her to hear the voice of Jesus in her life. She needs to know him, not just in that amazing moment of salvation, but daily, to have his comfort and encouragement, his strength in place of fear, his boldness in place of timidity.

The realisation for me was like a light going on in my head. The next part was simple. I needed to create a routine in my life to enable me to model this to my daughter. I needed to make a sacrifice. So often I keep things so comfortable that I don't really use or like that word 'sacrifice', but it's in this place of personal sacrifice that God strengthens faith and speaks.

The pattern I've developed is waking before my family which, if you have small children, you will know is early! It requires going to bed early, too, and now you're starting to see the sacrifice. To make the steps forward in my own faith I have had to sacrifice and shape routines. Going to bed early means I am able to get up an hour or more before my children and spend time listening to God myself, in prayer, in worship and in reading the Bible. God speaks and I listen. Then, from that place, I wake my eldest daughter before the rest of the family and read her a story from the Bible and pray with her and over her for her day.

Of course, this is just one model I am presenting to you. You can go and find a way that works for you and your family. But the essential ingredient is your relationship with the Lord and teaching your children to listen and respond to Jesus' voice.

Why bother? Let's be very honest and clear: the world will not teach your children to hear and trust the voice of Jesus! If you're counting on that, then know this: you're making an eternal mistake. Be ready to do battle for your children. The battle will be over your comfort, your apathy, you willingness to make sacrifices and to be in it for the long game; to be the father who teaches and knows what it means to listen and respond to Jesus.

EXPLORE . . .

Take some time to read about Samuel's encounter with the Lord and quietly reflect on this, asking Jesus to speak to you today.

How are you at listening? List a few times when you have noticed that listening has made a difference to you or to someone else.

_____

_____

_____

_____

_____

In what ways do you think your child/children need to be shown how to listen to the voice of Jesus?

_____

_____

_____

_____

_____

How can you start to help them listen and respond to Jesus as they grow?

_____

_____

_____

_____

_____

Try to write your own prayer or pledge to help you focus on helping your child/children listen to and know the voice of the Lord.

_____

_____

_____

_____

_____

PRAYER . . .

Lord, help me to hear and know your voice, to be ready to obey you and follow you wherever you may be calling me to go. Lead me, Jesus, and shape my life as I continue to unreservedly surrender all things into your hands. Amen.

14. Blended Families... Goodnight, John Boy

By Steve Legg

Step-parenting – it's not the Waltons. As I sit down to write this, my eldest daughter is waking up at her mum's house, on the sofa. And she's not talking to me. Or if she is, it's unrepeatable.

I can't write an article on step-parenting and pretend that we're some model family who join together in song as we sit holding hands in front of a log fire. It's just not like that.

It most definitely is not the Waltons. The truth is, the stakes are high in any family, any parenting situation, but they feel doubly high in a stepfamily.

The scope for second-guessing every decision you make is magnified because there are at least twice as many extended family members involved, each with their own view. Sometimes they are almost willing you to get it wrong. Parenting is hard and step-parenting has extra challenges, but my wife Bekah and I have learned a lot of lessons along the way that have proved invaluable.

GET REAL

Stepfamily life has its challenges and if you go into it expecting it to be the Waltons, reality will bite at some point and it will hurt. Setting realistic expectations is crucial. Know that it's going to be hard; that sometimes your kids or your partner's kids are going to kick back at you. Know that sometimes you'll get it wrong.

But know, too, that everybody gets it wrong sometimes. Everybody. They just don't tend to talk about it. That doesn't make you the worst parent in the world.

HONOUR THEIR MOTHER AND FATHER

This is the golden rule for step-parents, probably any parents, but especially step-parents: never, ever criticise the kid's mum or dad – ever. Just don't go there. Not even if your kids are doing it. Not even if they deserve it. Just don't do it.

When you criticise your child's other parent, you force them to choose between the two of you. If you make it clear how much you dislike their mum, you make it disloyal for them to like her. If you tell them their father is an idiot, then you make them an idiot for loving him. It puts pressure on kids that they should never have to handle. And kids aren't stupid. You don't need to spell it out, they are experts in reading us. They've been studying us since they were born. So be real. Don't just say the right things, get your attitude towards your ex sorted.

PRAY

On many levels this seems like an obvious one, but I mean *really* pray. Pray for your kids, one by one. Pray for your ex and your ex's new partner. There may be times when the words stick in your throat, or you feel tempted to send up prayers that request less than holy solutions to your problems.

But those are the days when you need to tell God about how you feel, then ask him to bless and love the people that seem to be making your life impossible. The thing about praying for a person is that it makes you see them in a different light. As we pray, we see how God sees them, and something in us softens.

LOVE AT ALL TIMES

Children need love. Above everything else in the world they need to know that they are loved with a love that knows no end. But that will mean different things for each of them. What it never means – and hear this loud and clear – is lavishing money on them. It's about learning their love language. If you don't know what I'm talking about, google it and buy the book.

My kids are all different. I have five girls and each of them needs something different from me. The youngest knows she is loved so long as she can have snuggles on the sofa. The next one up is all about quality time, which means I have to turn off my phone and give her my full attention. Next is words of affirmation – my middle daughter holds onto every bit of praise she has ever been given and stores it up like treasure. The eldest two are different again. One loves to be taken care of and the other feels precious when she's given a little gift.

They're all different.

I can't treat them the same because it wouldn't work. But however you show it, never withhold it, not when they're grumpy, not when they're rude, not when they're in trouble at school, not even when they tell you they hate you, and definitely not because they don't share your genes!

If you fall into the mistaken belief that love is an emotion, you'll fail with that last one. Love is an action. It's what we do. It means we have to try. Sometimes that means making the most enormous effort with kids that we don't have a blood-bond with. But it's always worth that effort.

HAVE FIRM, PADDED BOUNDARIES

Love is the key, but sometimes it needs to be firm. Our job is to raise kids who will be great adults; to teach them to be brave, strong, kind and selfless. Lots of this must happen through role modelling, but if we don't lay down firm boundaries with our children that have real consequences attached when they break them, we make their future uncertain. If we teach kids that they don't have to pull their weight or that they can treat us like dirt and yet still get everything done for them, they are going to get pretty hurt in the future when they discover that no one else will accept that in a relationship.

EQUAL BUT DIFFERENT

When you're a step-parent, you may have some children with your genes as well as those with someone else's. This cannot change how you treat them. They all need to feel loved and they all need to know their boundaries. But some need you to be their dad in a different way. Actually, in my family, I think all my girls need a dad, but their needs from my wife are different.

It sounds complicated. It is.

Bekah's kids see their real dad once, maybe twice a year. They therefore need me to be a dad to them too, because there is a big hole in their life without me. My kids spend half the week with their real mum. They have a mum already, so they don't need or want another. Bekah has had to learn what they do require from her, all the while continuing to lead the family with me and have authority in the home.

It's a minefield, but minefields, with time, patience and preferably a sniffer dog, can be crossed. Sometimes you get it wrong, there's an explosion, and it is painful, but you get up again. You move forward and eventually you get to the other side.

UNITED WE STAND, DIVIDED WE FALL

You have to have your partner's back. Don't undermine them. Kids can be masters at playing parents off against each other and that's even easier when they can pull the 'she's not my mum' card. But they won't do it if you don't play along.

Together you need to work out your house rules. That's not necessarily going to be easy. You will have often done things differently in the past. Take the time to reach some agreement and then stick to your plan as you follow it through with your kids. You're going to disagree sometimes with how the other handled things, but don't have that discussion in front of the kids; chat it through when you're on your own. You have to be each other's champions.

KNOW YOUR ROOTS

One of the things that has perhaps taken us the longest time to learn is that although we are one family, we are also two. It is good sometimes to create time to be the 'old gang'. Bekah and her girls occasionally end up home alone for the weekend when my girls are with their mum and I'm away working. It's time they treasure. They want us all to come home soon, but they've discovered that, actually, it's nice occasionally to be just like old times. And that's OK.

It made us realise that we needed to create the same kind of time, just once or twice a year, for me and my girls, to let them know that although we're one big family, the old bonds really matter. It usually just involves some walks on the beach, a trip to the kebab shop and sharing some good old memories, but it's important.

It's important because in the process of loving everybody equally, having the same boundaries and having your partner's back, your kids need to know that they haven't been replaced. You share a history. You've weathered things together. That shouldn't be neglected in the experiences of a new family.

As I said, it's a minefield, but it's a beautiful minefield. I've always maintained that when I married Bekah I got three for the price of one, and I meant it. I know she feels the same. We wouldn't change a thing. Our family is complicated but glorious, and who wants to be the Waltons anyway?

Steve Legg

Steve Legg is based in Littlehampton and has spent the last twenty-seven years on the road using a crazy mix of magic and comedy to communicate the Christian message. He is also the founding editor of Sorted *magazine and is married to Bekah, and together they have five daughters.*

15. Being A Dad to Teenagers

By Carl Beech

Being a dad to two teenage daughters brings the odd challenge. I used to think that the toddler phase was demanding and, prior to that, being a nappy-changing factory wasn't that much of a laugh if I'm being totally honest. But teenage girls? That's a tough gig. Sure, we have a lot of laughs and we all get on just great. But having to watch chick flicks? That takes it to another level. My insistence that *Rocky II* is really a love story just hasn't washed.

Then there's the problems of boys, fashion, make-up, hair, and the fact that they are both strong-minded, independent types who have an extensive range of opinions on nearly everything. The latter isn't so much of a problem as I've raised them to be that way and I like it. It's just, well, challenging.

The challenge that tops all the above hands down, however, is the problem of present-buying for Christmas and birthdays. What on earth does a dad get teenage girls? That's where my wife comes in, of course. She who knows the mystery of New Look, earrings and hair straighteners. Whoever knew that there were so many different types of hair straightener and that there is a premium brand that do the job of straightening better than all the others? To me it's as mysterious and confusing as quantum mechanics! Speaking of which: apparently, according to quantum mechanics, an electron can be in two places at once – something my wife Karen has been able to achieve for a long time and could have told you about way before the scientific community got on the case.

But back to presents . . . Every year since the stone age there have been 'must have' presents. In 1952 it was Mr Potato Head. One million of these kits were sold. Yes, it was a kit. Plastic arms, legs and a face. They didn't even give you a potato! In 1975 it was the pet rock, which was basically a rock in a box. Five million units sold. In 1983 it was the Cabbage Patch Doll. You can still visit BabyLand General Hospital to this day! Moving into the Eighties we had Transformers. In 1989 the Gameboy. In 1998 The Furby (40 million sold by 2000). In 2006 it was the PS3 and in 2009 the Zhu Zhu (basically a hamster with a battery – pretty similar to the real thing minus the vet bills, smells and the need to clean the cage). Genius.

Toy manufacturers know that parents will go to alarming lengths to buy little Timmy or little Suzy the gift of a lifetime, which will be discarded within a year as the new wonder toy pops along.

Why I am thinking about this? Because as I sit on my sofa, directly opposite me is a cheap, bright orange, inflatable basketball that came out of a box of Christmas crackers a couple of months ago. It's been a revelation. My fourteen-year-old daughter hasn't stopped taking it around the house with her, playing catch with me across the house at every given opportunity and chucking it at my head when I'm sitting down, reading the news. It's left me with a burning thought. Not, 'Why did I agonise over what to get them as a Christmas gift when I could have spent 35p on an inflatable basketball?' More like, 'When all is said and done, all my daughters really want is time with me. So why don't I make sure I'm fully present when they are present?'

Frankly, when my girls were little I could've taken them to the other side of the world for a holiday but, in all honesty, all they wanted was a swing and their dad to push them on it. They want you during these early years but – and read this very carefully – they need you even more when they are teenagers.

Now that my girls are teenagers they carve out their own time and often disappear into their rooms (pits) for hours at a time. I'm grateful, however, that they emerge to chat and talk through stuff that's on their minds with Karen and me on a regular basis. I put this down partly to the fact that during their early years we didn't have mobile phones to distract us or the phenomenon that is social media. Instead we played imaginary games, board games, hide-and-seek, had picnics, took walks, went swimming and basically enjoyed a lot of face-to-face contact with never a computer screen to distract us.

That's half the battle then: they still engage with us as teens. But the next bit is trickier! How do we handle some of the things they share with us and how do we keep them close? We live in complex, challenging times and our kids are under pressures we weren't subjected to with the same intensity. Drugs, cyberbullying, promiscuity on an epic scale . . . I could go on! Well, my advice is simply this:

- Be prepared to listen and not judge.
- Negotiate and don't prescribe unless you need to.
- Pray daily for them, including for stuff like future relationships.
- Be the same person at church as you are at home.
- Treat your wife with the same honour and respect that you would want a man to give to your daughter.
- Put the phone down.
- Make eye contact when they are talking.
- Apologise when you get things wrong.
- Be prepared to give ground.
- Where you have fixed boundaries, stick to them. Consistency is key!
- Buy a cheap ball and play catch.

Keeping the lines of communication open with teenagers is completely different to toddlers. But don't think that as a dad to daughters you can't talk about sex, men, emotions, hormones, hair and clothes. You can and you must and your kids will be all the better for it. You'll only get there, though, if you start to work on it when they are toddlers. It's a tough gig but let's give it our best shot.

Carl Beech
CVM President

16. Trust – Abba Father (Daddy)

If you are like me, when you get a book you might attempt to annoy those around you who have recommended it to you by turning immediately to the back page to see how it all ends. Well, if you have just done that, welcome to the main point!

God has provided a way for you and for me to know him, the perfect Father, and to learn from him how to be fathered and how to pass that on and more. The way to God is open to us because of what Jesus was able to do and this is the best news ever.

As a younger man I was raised as a Christian, but whilst I had all the head knowledge to live a life of faith, trusting God, I wouldn't allow it to hit my heart. Why? Well I wanted to be the master of my own destiny: my time, my money, my life and my choices. I was a bit like the fictional children's character He-Man.

If you have ever seen He-Man you will know where I am going with this. He was at the peak of physical excellence and brandished a sword that sent his enemies fleeing in sheer terror. He also had auburn hair that was salon fresh, but the point is, he was He-Man, Master of the Universe!

I started to realise that I was trying to be He-Man, the master of my own universe and Jesus had something to say about it.

The Bible shows me that Jesus asks me to trust him, to follow him and let him be the master of my universe. In truth, I was afraid to let go of the controls just in case it didn't work. But

I did, and Jesus is shaping me to be the man I know I want to be – a man like him: self-controlled, disciplined, passionate, full of mercy, grace and forgiveness.

The deal is, there are two invites here and we mustn't ignore either. The first is to trust Jesus with who you are, all your failings, dreams, hopes, passions, the lot. Invite him into your heart, acknowledging where you have been in your life until now, and where you can start to go with Jesus in your life.

Secondly, it is important that you don't miss the cost. There is an invite here for you to accept not only Jesus, but the cost of following him. To place your life into his hands and keep it there will cost you. Integrity and holiness are part of the package, surrender and obedience are in the small print. Adventure, freedom, joy, peace, forgiveness and hope for tomorrow are all included, but you can't afford to miss the invite to count the cost too.

Jesus isn't calling men to fill churches on a Sunday, but then shut the door on him from Monday to Saturday. He is calling us to follow him at home, work and even when we are with our mates!

This book has been about founding fathers, establishing fathers who really give of themselves to raise up and help children be loved and cared for by fathers. As fathers we can know that investment in our own lives too. You might not have that earthly experience, perhaps it was terrible or missed, but you and I can have this spiritual heavenly Father who will never fail us. He will shape our lives and teach us. He will be closer to you than you can imagine and he can use our lives for the most amazing works.

If you are ready to embrace the life of adventure that is following Jesus, pray the prayer below.

PRAYER . . .

Jesus, thank you for going to the cross for me and that your life has set me free. Help me to turn from my old ways and follow you. Help me to always count the cost, to love and trust you with my life. By the Holy Spirit, be the master of my universe, Jesus, and shape me into the man I long to be. Amen.

GET IN TOUCH...

CVM

The Hub

Unit 2 Dunston Road

Chesterfield

S41 8XA

Tel: 01246 452483

BE SOCIAL:

 https://www.facebook.com/CVMen

 https://twitter.com/cvmen

 https://www.youtube.com/user/CVMmedia

 https://vimeo.com/cvmmedia